DARK ROUX

LET IT BE A DARK ROUX

New and Selected Poems

Sheryl St. Germain

Autumn House Press

PITTSBURGH

"Autumn House" and "Autumn House Press" are registered trademarks
owned by Autumn House Press, a non-profit corporation whose mission
is the publication and promotion of poetry and other fine literature.

Autumn House Press Staff
Executive Editor and Founder: Michael Simms
Executive Director: Richard St. John
Community Outreach Director: Michael Wurster
Co-Director: Eva-Maria Simms
Fiction Editor: Sharon Dilworth
Special Projects Coordinator: Joshua Storey
Associate Editors: Anna Catone, Laurie Mansell Reich
Editorial Consultant: Ziggy Edwards
Media Consultant: Jan Beatty
Tech Crew Chief: Michael Milberger
Intern: Laura Crawford

ISBN: 978-1-932870-16-9
Library of Congress Control Number:

All Autumn House books are printed on acid-free paper and meet the
international standards of permanent books intended for purchase by
libraries.

Acknowledgments

I would like to express gratitude to the presses and journals below that published versions of many of these poems. Special thanks to those who have nurtured my spirit over the years: Joe Ahearn, John Biguenet, Darrell Bourque, Tim Gautreaux, Greg Guirard, Bob Hass, Brenda Hillman, Galway Kinnell, Alexis Levitin, Debra Marquart, Robin Metz, Sharon Olds, Rainer Schulte, Tim Seibles, Derek Smith and Patty Turner. I am especially indebted to the Squaw Valley Community of Writers and to Joe and Lucianne Carmichael of A Studio in the Woods for providing a nourishing community, and to Stanley Barkan and Chuck Taylor for their early confidence in my abilities. I am also grateful to the Texas Institute of Letters and UT Austin for their sponsorship of the Dobie-Paisano Fellowship, to the National Endowment for the Arts for two fellowships that provided me with time and resources to complete many of these poems, and to Chatham University for a Central Research Fund award.

The Journals of Scheherazade. Denton: University of North Texas Press, 1996.
How Heavy the Breath of God. Denton: University of North Texas Press, 1994. Second edition, 1995.
Making Bread at Midnight. Austin: Slough Press, 1992. Second edition, with afterword, 1995.
Going Home. Van Nuys: Perivale Press, 1989. Second printing, 1990.
The Mask of Medusa. New York: Cross Cultural Press, 1987. Second printing, 1989.

Versions of some of these poems appeared in *The Abiko Quarterly, The American Literary Review, Bloomsbury Review, Bitterroot, Breaking Ground, Calyx, Chile Verde, Cimmaron Review, Crab Orchard Review, Cream City Review, The Dallas Review, Five A.M., Five Fingers Review, Footwork, Graham House Review, The Guadalupe Review, High Plains Literary Review, Louisiana Literature, Luna, Massachusetts Review, Negative Capability, New Letters, No Roses Review, OnTheBus, The Oxford American, RiverSedge, River Styx, Spoon River Poetry Review, The Texas Review, Triquarterly, Vortex* and *Women's Studies Quarterly.*

The Autumn House Poetry Series

**Michael Simms,
Executive Editor**

*Snow White Horses, Selected
Poems 1973-88* by Ed Ochester

*The Leaving, New and Selected
Poems* by Sue Ellen Thompson

Dirt by Jo McDougall

Fire in the Orchard by Gary
Margolis

*Just Once, New and Previous
Poems* by Samuel Hazo

The White Calf Kicks by
Deborah Slicer ● 2003, selected
by Naomi Shihab Nye

The Divine Salt by Peter Blair

The Dark Takes Aim by Julie
Suk

Satisfied with Havoc by Jo
McDougall

Half Lives by Richard Jackson

Not God After All by Gerald
Stern (with drawings by Sheba
Sharrow)

Dear Good Naked Morning
by Ruth L. Schwartz ● 2004,
selected by Alicia Ostriker

A Flight to Elsewhere by Samuel
Hazo

Collected Poems by Patricia
Dobler

*The Autumn House Anthology of
Contemporary American Poetry*,
edited by Sue Ellen Thompson

Déjà Vu Diner by Leonard
Gontarek

Lucky Wreck by Ada Limon ●
2005, selected by Jean Valentine

The Golden Hour by Sue Ellen
Thompson

Woman in the Painting by
Andrea Hollander Budy

*Joyful Noise: An Anthology of
American Spiritual Poetry*, edited
by Robert Strong

No Sweeter Fat by Nancy Pagh ●
2006, selected by Tim Seibles

*Unreconstructed: Poems Selected
and New* by Ed Ochester

Rabbis of the Air by Philip
Terman

*Let It Be a Dark Roux: New and
Selected Poems* by Sheryl
St. Germain

Dixmont by Rick Campbell

The River Is Rising by Patricia
Jabbeh Wesley

● winner of the annual Autumn
House Press Poetry Prize

Contents

OVERTURE

3   Flambeau Carriers

from **THE MASK OF MEDUSA** (1987)

7   Medusa in Southern Louisiana
8   Becoming Medusa
9   Medusa Visits New York City in Winter
10   Medusa Looks Out Her Window in January
11   Medusa Dreams of Red Tulips

from **GOING HOME** (1989)

15   Going Home: New Orleans
17   The Lake
18   Things My Mother Always Told Me
20   Mother's Red Beans and Rice
22   Hot Sauce
24   Making a Roux
25   Scars
26   Getting Up Out the Water
27   Curry
28   Undressing

from **MAKING BREAD AT MIDNIGHT** (1992)

33   My Mother's Perfume
35   Addiction
37   Overdose
38   Looking for Fossils
40   The Second Coming
41   Hurricane Season
42   The Father the House Built
43   Alcoholic

45 Fanks
46 Deathbed
47 Day of the Dead
48 Grief
49 Some Months After My Father's Death
50 Cajun
51 Cleaning a Fish for the First Time
54 Too Late, for My Fingers
56 Eating
57 On Taking a Child to My Bed
58 Wanting to Be Mary Magdalene
60 First Summer in Nice
62 Eating Raspberries

from **HOW HEAVY THE BREATH OF GOD** (1994)

67 Looking for Grace in Ecuador
68 Street Market, Otavalo
72 Why I Went into the Jungle
73 What the Sea Turtles Know
75 In the Garden of Eden
76 Big Fish
77 Fisherman
78 The Headlights of God
79 Losing Faith
81 Building for War
82 Flooded Crossing
83 August Fire
85 The Erotic
86 Want
87 Just Say No to Insect Sex
89 Blindfolds, Ropes
90 Angels

from **THE JOURNALS OF SCHEHERAZADE** (1996)

95   My Body in Summer
97   Rent
100   Pain Killers
102   Hacking Away the Wisteria
104   Thinking About Being a Woman as I Drive from Louisiana
         to New Mexico
109   Sestina for the Beloved
      from "Eight Nights of Fantasies"
111   The First Night: the Invitation
113   The Eighth Night: in the Galapagos Islands

NEW POEMS

117   Snow Storm
118   Snow, Six Months Sober
119   Midwestern
120   Winter Solstice
121   Promise of Snow
122   A Few Days After the Attack
123   Wild Ones
124   Night
127   The Night Before I Left for Seattle
128   Tinnitus

A SUITE FOR NEW ORLEANS

135   Night Parade
136   Jazz Sax
137   Speaking About Loss
138   What We Found in Our Mother's Shed After the Hurricane
139   Carnival: an Ode to New Orleans
143   Bread Pudding with Whiskey Sauce
146   Getting Rid of the Accent
148   Joy

for Gray,
always

When your father lies
in the last light
and your mother cries for him,
listen to the sound of her crying.
When your father dies
take notes
somewhere inside.

If there is a heaven
he will forgive you
if the line you found was a good one.

It does not have to be worth the dying.

—*Miller Williams, "Let Me Tell You"*

OVERTURE

Flambeau Carriers

Red-eyed and sweating whiskey,
they were the true gods of the night,
and I loved to watch them carry
their precious signs of fire,

I loved the way they would lurch
and stagger, mambo, shuffle,
zigzag their way down
the street, showing off fire

like bright words or wounds,
diamond drops of it falling
to the ground like sweat,
torch and carrier so united
it seemed as if the carriers themselves
were made of fire.

I think I loved them because
even as a child I sensed that
the poems I struggled to write
in the dark of my bedroom
were like this,
                    drunken
epiphanies of light,
          stuttering
moments between
the floats of Dream and Nightmare,

I think I loved them because
I wanted this to be the poet's job:
to carry the burning night,
to hold high our stumbling,
astonished,
street-dancing selves.

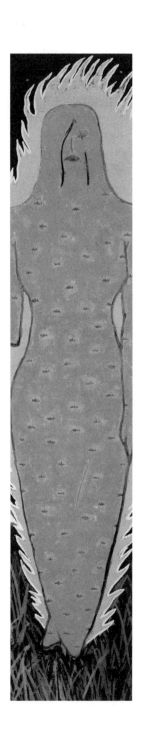

THE
MASK OF
MEDUSA

1987

Medusa in Southern Louisiana

Look down upon these fingers of bayous,
Spanish moss curled like gray snakes
crowning thick-breasted oaks
and you will see me.

You'll find me in the river
they call Blood,
you'll find me in stagnant waters
where cypress trees bare their roots
and cry out for sky. My voice
comes from here, this drowned crater
that pulls everything into it.

Listen for my whisper
in the warm southern nights,
listen for my scream
in the crowded black waters.

Becoming Medusa

Today I have sung myself to my children, they have nursed at my breasts with hungry mouths, played naked in the heat of my hips, and I have opened my legs, without speaking, to my husband. It is the silence of my voice that keeps this family alive and together. But tonight as I lie alone in the room, my thighs scream and I feel my hair crawling with snakes. I gather the darkness into the shape of a man, I screech my desire and we fuck until I feel blood in my head again. My sisters arrive and we fly like crows out of this house. We are looking for a language, we are looking for diamonds to steal, diamonds in the shape of words, diamonds that speak lies about us, we want to take them, to smash them, to eat the splinters and pass them out of our bodies. We cut our names into books of history, and we empty file cabinets that contain stories of us we haven't written. In one night we destroy everything. In one night we spend ourselves. I fly home, and in the hours before the cry of the first child I nurse myself, fingering the wound that is always fresh—this slit, this split, this opening between my days and nights. I enter my skin once again with needle and thread, pull, tighten, and pull again. I am sutured for the day.

Medusa Visits New York City in Winter

I've walked for hours watching steam billow, cloud
and rise from the grated mouths of unfamiliar streets.
I've walked for hours thinking of nothing but love,
and how much I want it, a want I can taste,
a want that flavors the cold breaths I take in,
that turns the breaths warm and wet in my mouth.
I've walked for hours thinking of how I might
rid myself of these eyes that think they are vultures,
these eyes that attack lovers as if they were cadavers
waiting to be picked clean.

These streets are full of people like me:
people walking with absence carved
into their sides, an absence that defines
what is not there, an absence that rains
down on them, falls off onto the streets
that glisten like sweating skin.
But when I look everyone turns to ice,
their stopped gestures of greeting
as incomprehensible as the street's caught breath.

Medusa Looks Out Her Window in January

Dead winter is my season, when trees pose
stiff and naked for the camera,
leafless, but not breathless—
with breath held
in for a moment, they stand
etched in to the sky. It's comforting
that they never move.
And I'm beginning to think
that there's beauty in even this,

in these still trees, and this white
moon cut and pasted
to the black paper night,
this moon that never grows or shrinks.
Everything in its light holds
its breath.
                            And let me tell you
there is more life in this still
held breath than in the madness of spring,
because for just a moment
movement toward death is stopped.

Who knows if we will ever
be able to gather our strength
to take in another breath.
Hold it,
hold it while you can.

Medusa Dreams of Red Tulips

If someone could love me as I am
I would take off my face
I would undress my snakes
peel back their raw skin
change them into red tulips
I would wear the red tulips as a crown
I would go with the one who loved me to dance
the red tulips would spin with us and away from us
the red tulips would bring us together again

We would dance all night
his breath on my neck and lips would be cool
as the new blood between my legs would be warm
his breath my blood the room would be night red
the red tulips would grow and cradle us

Later the red tulips would gulp water from a glass by the bed
and he would drink from my breasts with a great thirst
the tulips are ancient his mouth would speak
through my nipples in a language I knew
before I was born

I dream of red tulips lying in disarray on white sheets
red tulips bruised and breathing underneath us
the one who loved me would place a barely opened bud
between my thighs
he would wrap a long leg around me
like a green vine
we would begin to blossom

We would not think about my face and the snakes
guarding the door
waiting for the dream to end

GOING
HOME

1989

Going Home: New Orleans

for my grandmother, Theresa Frank

Some slow evenings when the light hangs late and stubborn in the sky,
gives itself up to darkness slowly and deliberately, slow cloud after
   slow cloud,
slowness enters me like something familiar,
and it feels like going home.

It's all there in the disappearing light:
all the evenings of slow sky and slow loving, slow boats on
   sluggish bayous;
the thick-middled trees with the slow-sounding names—oak,
   mimosa, pecan, magnolia;
the slow tree sap that sticks in your hair when you lie with the trees;
and the maple syrup and pancakes and grits, the butter melting
slowly into and down the sides like sweat between breasts of sloe-eyed
   strippers;
and the slow-throated blues that floats over the city like fog;
and the weeping, the willows, the cut onions, the cayenne, the
   slow-cooking beans with marrow-thick gravy;
and all the mint juleps drunk so slowly on all the slow southern
   porches,
the bourbon and sugar and mint going down warm and brown,
   syrup and slow;
and all the ice cubes melting in all the iced teas,
all the slow-faced people sitting in all the slowly rocking rockers;
and the crabs and the shrimp and crawfish, the hard shells
slowly and deliberately and lovingly removed, the delicate flesh
slowly sucked out of heads and legs and tails;
and the slow lips that eat and drink and love and speak
that slow luxurious language, savoring each word like a long-
   missed lover;
and the slow-moving nuns, the black habits dragging the swollen
   ground;

and the slow river that cradles it all, and the chicory coffee
that cuts through it all, slow-boiled and black as dirt;
and the slow dreams and the slow-healing wounds and the slow
  smoke of it all
slipping out, ballooning into the sky—slow, deliberate, and
  magnificent.

The Lake

I think it was always polluted,
even as a child I remember that gray-peppered foam
mouthing the shore. Some days it had a rotten smell to it,
especially hot days when the fish that had tried so hard
to filter the shit through their gills gave up
and floated open-eyed to the surface.
I used to be amazed at what could thrive in that lake,
scavengers, shellfish, how white and sweet their meat was.
Its name was French like mine: *Pontchartrain,*
St. Germain, and the names echo each other nights
when I feel those waters rising, and the dead fish all rise up,
the dark waters swelling higher and higher
until I have to give it up or drown,
swim for whatever hard-shelled goodness I can find.

Things My Mother Always Told Me

1. Always Wear Clean Underwear, You Never Know
When You Might Get in a Car Accident

She always slightly missed the point, my mother, like a woman
who can't tell the difference between lust and love, marries
the one she lusts after, thinks her love affairs trivial—
I never wore underwear, though she gave it to me year
after year, cotton and silk lace panties blue and pink,
white and clean as death.
I'd throw a pair in the dirty clothes every other day
so she'd think I was wearing them, but I never
wore them, no, I was afraid to get
in a car accident if I did, and besides,
if I did get in a car accident
I would want them to find me dead
as I was alive, the wind rushing up my legs under
my skirt, everything open
and frank as the highway,
not smothered and sad by underwear;
I would want them to find me
bare-assed and bleeding,
spread out on the street.

*2. Don't Bite Your Fingernails, Think Where Those
Fingers Have Been*

It's not the biting so much
as the taste of fingers in the mouth
clean or dirty, the particular smell
of a lover's skin from the night before,
newspaper ink black with blood from the day's news,
the smells that stay on the fingers like finger
paint, smells that linger into the night caught
in the place between skin and nail, where
grit fills the nail dark with life
and soap clings white and hopeless for days
after washing.
This is the world become body,
you can only taste it
if your nails are short, this im-
perfection, this bit of hard skin
suckled and bitten off, this small
intimacy with yourself.

Mother's Red Beans and Rice

The beans were tight and small as my young ass,
and I loved the sound they made when she poured them
into the pot. I could never resist plunging
both my hands in to feel the abundance of them,
the hardness and sureness of them.
In the morning, after she'd left them to soak
in the night, they would feel different—larger,
softer, the skins wrinkled like her stomach
from all the children.

She'd put them on to cook, adding to them
as the beans heated—ham bone with marrow
to make the gravy thick,
salt pork to make them meaty, smoky.

She'd scavenge around for whatever else we had,
always an onion or two, and I'd watch her
as she chopped them—I knew it was the onions
made her cry, but I also knew there was much
to cry about, so I was glad when she finished,
scraped the onion off the cutting board
and into the pot.

She always took so long cutting up the garlic,
mincing and mincing, and not really paying attention
until her eyes became dreamy and sloppy like they did
when she talked about the boy she almost married,
and inevitably she would cut a thumb or index finger,
and bits of garlic would turn pink from drops of blood,
and I would turn white—there was something horrible
about my mother's blood, it was too red, obscenely red,

so red it was almost
black. She'd bandage the finger,
gather all the garlic up,
throw it in the pot.

The beans would cook all day, filling the house
with their creamy onion pork smell, the sauce slowly
thickening, the beans slowly softening.

The beans were always good,
and when I make them now sadness falls over me
like a fleece, the sharp bean smells fill my lungs
like the smoke or blood of her—

I eat them like joy.

Hot Sauce

Mother wasn't the one who convinced us it was good,
though we could all see she loved it.
She'd splatter her morning eggs
with the red kind so they looked bloody,
riddled with bullet holes;
she'd put it on any sandwich,
beans, rice, gumbo, salad—
nothing escaped the shaking of the hot sauce bottle.
Nights when daddy would come home late,
hands and words flailing,
she'd go to the kitchen after he'd slunk off
to his sleep and make something to eat,
anything at all, just to have something
to put hot sauce on.

We didn't understand
how she could stand so much hot,
how she could really like it.
She kept offering it to us meal after meal
but we wouldn't take any: we knew
it was hot.

It was daddy who got us to like it,
who thought of it as punishment
when we got too old for whipping.
He'd have us stick out our tongues
like we did for the priest at Communion,
and he'd shake three or four drops of the stuff
on them. We would lie afterwards in our beds
curled up, nursing tongues, lips, the roofs of mouths—
it seemed all that was alive of us was that burning.

And that was how it happened,
one day when I stuck out my tongue
and he splattered the red drops on it
I closed my mouth and I liked it,
I closed my mouth and it felt familiar,
and from then on I didn't mind it so much,

the sauce, the hot.

24

Making a Roux

I am making a roux, like my mother, like my grand-
mother, like all the women whose shadows stretch
before and behind me. I am standing before the stove
stirring, and I wonder what they thought of as they stood
and stirred, as their hands went round and round
in this ancient gesture. I wonder
if they looked deep into it as I do, as if it could speak,
stared at this flour and grease come together,
this stuff that is base, thickener, nothing
you cook will ever cohere without it, this
stuff that must be cooked over the slowest fire,
this stuff that must be tended
until the heat turns it the color of nuts,
the color of the earth, the river,
the sweet color of some skins,
the color the roux gives up
to the dish it will thicken.

I am making a roux, like my mother, like my grand-
mother, it is so simple, this flour and grease
come together with its thick bready
flavor, like the two of us come together.
Let it be a good roux, a dark roux, let the cream,
the smoky glue, the sweat and dirt of us,
thicken some dish already seasoned,
already rich.

Scars

Today the streets run like gray scars
across the cold face of this city.

I love the scar on my stomach that runs fat
and long where they cut my son out;

I touch it at night sometimes, I like to feel
how the skin is different there, protruded and smooth

something happened here
the body heals itself, we change,

grow older, are not gods,
and a poem is a scar, not the wound

itself but the knowledge
of the wound, the flag

of the wound, a wiser tissue
laid out like a street, this way, this way.

Getting Up Out the Water

I love my legs, they are strong legs;
they are my mother's legs, big and well-formed,
the calves firm and muscled,
the thighs generous and solid except at the place
where they meet and soften;
and my hips and buttocks, full, rounded and strong
for moving my legs, for the pleasure of children and lovers;
and my feet, they are large feet to carry my body,
with strong ankles, and even my toes are well shaped and strong.
And I love my arms too, shoulders and forearms,
good for cradling and carrying,
and my wrists and hands; they are my father's hands
that know song and stretch, to hold a thing firmly and gently.

And when I grasp the handle of the rope and lie back in the water
and when I am pulled up, the water rushes between my legs,
and I am rushing into the wind toward the hot blue sun,
opening my mouth and shouting because I know my body is ready
for anything, for breaking the wake, for the unpolished water;
because I am holding on with all my proud female strength,
with finger and wrist and forearm and shoulders,
with feet and ankle and calf and thigh I am holding on
with all the good grit of this body.

Curry

I bring each one to you after I grind it,
still in the mortar, warm and pungent you
lie there on the sofa watching me; I look
at you as I grind each spice,
feel your eyes stippling the back of my legs
and neck. I turn to your eyes again and again:
they know what I can do with these spices—
garlic and ginger, turmeric and abundant
red pepper—I grind them together, mix them
into yogurt white as my camisole,
rub the chicken pieces with the spiced yogurt,
yellow from the turmeric and red pepper.
I pierce the skin with a fork, leave the kitchen
to go to you in the next room, to rub
my hands of spiced yogurt and raw chicken
on your chest and thighs. I want to pierce you,
I want my hands to be full of you, of your eyes
pretending a rope is wrapped around arms and legs,
pretending all you can do is look at me
in just this camisole, and the fresh-ground pepper—

Our voices whisper what we will do
when we finish; our voices are cumin
and coriander, mustard seed and nutmeg,
cilantro, saffron and cinnamon;
just-crushed cardamom and allspice, almonds
and onions, shredded coconut, butter and cloves,
lemon, and your eyes that meet mine as I take off
the camisole, and the rubbed chicken and Marsala
begin to heat up, all the spices mingling,
pepper-rich, blood-thick.

Undressing

It has to do with dressing and undressing, he said.
The boots sound black and sharp on the stairs
as the woman walks up. The house is cold;
she walks over to turn the heat on,
the wood floor shouts at each step.

It has to do with dressing and undressing.
She pulls the boots off, sits on the edge of the bed,
slips her earrings off, remembers how
he liked to do this, how long it would take him
to get one out, to lay the ear completely bare.
She drops them one at a time onto the dresser.
The deep clicks, like the clucking of a tongue when they hit,
startle her for a moment. But no one is here,
except for the room, and the sounds,
and it is the room—which is large—that largens
the sounds until they are larger than what made them.
She pulls the pins from her hair next.
Their tinny bits of sound thin through the air,
and her hair falls down around like a muttering let loose.

Dressing and undressing.
She pulls her shirt off, skirt, stockings.
The crotch smells heavy, sweet, familiar.
She touches a finger to herself, she is
wet like the inside of a cut grape.
The cold makes the skin on her breasts rise;
she unhooks the bra and lets it fall.

It has to do with dressing.
She pulls a gown on, lies down
and wraps a blanket around like a thick word.

And undressing.

MAKING
BREAD AT
MIDNIGHT

1992

My Mother's Perfume

When she'd come to kiss us
good night, stockinged, girdled
and lipsticked, hair curled
and sprayed stiff as tulle,
her fragrance would fall over us
like a warm winter, a drug
that perfumed us to sleep—

the smells would come on like a melody,
first violin of jasmine,
bitter-flowered tea we used to drink,

vanilla, heavy and creamy,
thick tongued,
the dark-white velvet smell
of heating bottles of milk late at night—
if I stumbled into the kitchen
wanting a drink, I would see her
shaking milk from a nipple
onto her wrist and arm
to test its warmth—
and musk would seep out
under the vanilla, smell of civet,
a held cello note,
honey-new blood smell and young
sweat; cedar, the smell of forest,
of the chests my grandfather made
for us, of the way winter clothes
smelled the first day of fall, sandalwood
and vetiver, ylang-ylang, orris,
roots and flowers, grasses
whose names I didn't know then,
all I knew was they smelled foreign,
like incense shops or church altars
where candles burned.

And now I sometimes turn out the lights
and put on perfume as if it were her,
as if it were milk and my skin thirsting,
to wrists, thighs, neck, until

I am swollen with her, the whole orchestra
of her tortured wifehood, her gorgeous
ambiguity entering me like a drug
until I sleep and dream of another life.

Addiction

in memory of my brother, Jay St. Germain, 1958-1981

The truth is I loved it,
the whole ritual of it,
the way he would fist up his arm, then
hold it out so trusting and bare,
the vein pushed up all blue and throbbing
and wanting to be pierced,
his opposite hand gripped tight as death
around the upper arm,

the way I would try to enter the vein,
almost parallel to the arm,
push lightly but firmly, not
too deep,
you don't want to go through
the vein, just in,
then pull back until you see
blood, then

hold the needle very still, slowly
shoot him with it.
Like that I would enter him,
slowly, slowly, very still,
don't move,
then he would let the fist out,
loosen his grip on the upper arm—

and oh, the movement of his lips
when he asked that I open my arms.
How careful,
how good he was, sliding
the needle silver and slender
so easily into me, as though
my skin and veins were made for it,
and when he had finished, pulled

it out, I would be coming
in my fingers, hands, my ear lobes
were coming, heart, thighs,
tongue, eyes and brain were coming,
thick and brilliant as the last thin match
against a homeless bitter cold.

I even loved the pin-sized bruises,
I would finger them alone in my room
like marks of passion;
by the time they turned yellow,
my dreams were full of needles.

We both took lovers who loved
this entering and being entered,
but when he brought over the
pale-faced girl so full of needle holes
he had to lay her on her back

like a corpse and stick the needle
over and over in her ankle veins
to find one that wasn't weary
of all that joy, I became sick
with it, but

you know, it still stalks my dreams,
and deaths make no difference:
there is only the body's huge wanting.

When I think of my brother
all spilled out on the floor
I say nothing to anyone.
I know what it's like to want joy
at any cost.

Overdose

Mother herded us to church on Sundays,
sacrificed her teeth to send us to Catholic school,
but it didn't save my brother.

This is what I think as I watch him,
brainless in his young hospital bed.

Once my father took my brother's head
in his hands, as I guess fathers still do
with sons, and beat it against the kitchen door
telling him he was not God,
not God, was the opposite of God,
and knocked and pounded him to the door
with all the mean power of his life.
It is a knocking I cannot get out
of my own heart, a knocking I hear
in the deepest of sleeps.

This time is not my father's fault,
though who can know what pain
was overdosed.

The I.V. drips into the soul-
emptied body (the priests don't know
where the souls of the brain-dead go)
and I think of my father beating God
out of him, and I can hear God
goose-stepping the halls of the hospital
like a Nazi, refusing grace, refusing
forgiveness, his head full of plans
for the next Flood.

Looking for Fossils

When I found my brother
in the bed of the creek
I wasn't looking for him.

I was scraping for fossils,
sifting rock and pebble for some piece
that would distinguish itself,

a curl, a spiral, an unusual mark,
just some small shell or snail.
I wasn't surprised to see him, though,

when I felt his face in the detritus
I said *of course*. It was handsome,
as it had been in life, but smoother,

cool to the touch. In stone he had not aged.
I uncovered the rest of his body,
shoulder, chest, thighs, calves.

Even the track marks on his arms
had been preserved. Bulbous,
like feeding traces, the trails or burrows

of some ancient worm. I tried to cradle him,
happy he had not been eaten away,
his face disappeared to dust.

And now I scrape out a place next to him
in the hot rocks and lie down.
I wonder how long it will take—

my feet already hard with callous.
Will it be like that, something
to hardly notice.

The slope above us is pocked
with needle marks. The creek
spoons out scree like a drug.

The Second Coming

After my brother died I knew
that when Jesus came back
needle marks would gut his arms
like stigmata,
the crook of his arm
would be mapped
with 2000 years of dying.

All junkies become Jesus
when they die, which is why
they never really die,
so that when Jesus returns
it will be as my brother.
Thinner than I remember him
with hair grown long and thick,
and beard, he will lie crumpled
in a corner of a street.

I have never seen God
but I have seen the sad rapture
of those I love, their eyes
heavy with Him.
I have watched them hold out
their Jesus arms
and nail their Jesus veins,
and I have watched them hang
without salvation.

Hurricane Season

1

Those who have already been destroyed
recognize its signs: the sky
clouds like a glaucous eye,
the wind muscles over whatever
is weak. Waves swell, engorged
with too much of something.
A lashing, a swimming of tongues
through air. Birds disappear.
The smell of ocean in the wrong place,
of something diseased, lost fish.
The sky bellows, darkens, roars
like a drunk.

Those unacquainted with destruction
ask for wind speeds, amount of rainfall,
degree of movement. A plotting,
a computation of the destruction.

2

For some of us, all seasons are hurricane.
The winds gale up, working us like seed,
moving us like desire.

What lies beyond measurement
is all of beauty and terror.

To understand is to evacuate.

The Father the House Built

This is the father the house built.

This is the plastic cup of the father the house built.

These are the cubes of ice in the plastic cup of the father the house built.

This is the bottle of Scotch sitting next to the cubes of ice in the plastic cup of the father the house built.

This is the parking lot where the car sits with the plastic cup and the cubes of ice and the bottle of Scotch that belongs to the father the house built.

This is the father who drank the Scotch in the plastic cup with the cubes of ice in the car of the parking lot.

This is the drunk father
the father drunk
the drunk
the father
the house built
who built the house
and watched it fall.

Alcoholic

1

Each night when the weight of what we are
and what we might have been settles around the house,
rolling off backs like lies off tongues of caught children;
when all that is light becomes voice,
I huddle with my child, crook him under arm,
and read him stories.

We keep a mug of milk next to the bed, and between
stories pass it between us, drinking solemnly.
I read for a long time, until my voice becomes breast,
and his belly fat with milk and story.

He is comforted now as when all he knew was nipple;
the world has a shape, there are beginnings and endings,
there is some otherness that is benevolent. And I am comforted,
as when I first felt warm thread of nerve, muscle, and gland
contract and release milk to his mouth.
He lies now, as then, full; the milk is caught
in the corners of his mouth.

2

I am sitting next to my mother, she is reading me
the story of a girl who sells matches.
The girl is weary of all that is real—
of her shoelessness, of her feet, so thick and blue
they no longer bleed; of the father's hand
that knows too well where she still can feel;
of these matches no one wants.
She is weary of what the world has made of her,
and in that weariness before death comes a clarity

not unlike that moment when the body, after much effort,
can no longer fight off freezing and gives up:
nerves become numb, hands and feet seem warm for the first time.
In that moment she decides to light the matches
instead of sell them, and she fights it all off
with illuminations, hallucinations of suns and candles,
feasts, grandmothers, hands that love.

She lights them all,
she lets them catch and burn to her fingers.

3

Tonight my son wants to wear his grandfather's medals.
He asks me, again, what the medals were for,
and I know tonight I will tell stories about my father.
I am good at this. I find the one skimpy tree of truth,
decorate it so thickly that it is difficult to say
where is decoration and where is tree:
he saved thousands of people during the big hurricane,
our street was a river, he came in a boat,
he walked on water to save the people
stranded on housetops. *Did he save you too, mom?* he asks.
Yes, I say, caught in the telling, and my son is happy,
he will save people when he grows up,
he will be like this story of his grandfather.

And when my father dies and my son asks about his death,
I will be ready with the story of a man who drank stories
from a cup to fight something I cannot describe.
I will not tell him that stories are lies,
that tonight I understand my father
is killing himself. There is nothing to be done,
he has already begun to light the matches.

Fanks

He stopped there after work every day,
it's where he got the bar room smell
he carried around like some people
carry religion. The smoke hung thick
as grief in his clothes and hair,
and the beer announced his lips like a whistle
did a train.
I loved it when she'd send me
to fetch him from across the street;
the room would be full of beery dark
and bluster; the doors swung open
easy as sin even for a young girl
like me, and I'd find him happy, singing
or reciting some poem he'd got by heart.
He'd teach me a verse or two, give me a swig
from his mug, sparkling and bitter.

Deathbed

We are trying to make love, but my father keeps interfering.
Flat on your back there, eyes closed, sour breath,
you remind me of him; it is too soon to be trying
for some joy. I go on with it, though, making
the appropriate responses, willing my nipples erect.
I am dark and thick with my father, I moan with his lips,
breathe for him. I am drunk, I am his obscene mouth,
you are fucking my father, you don't care
that his children are watching,
that his wife cries the night red.
I thrust at you, anguished,
as if this thrusting could save or hurt you.
I grow slack with drink, sleep.

We are deaths apart in this bed.

Day of the Dead

1

October, the month of the swollen O,
the month of the faces of the dead,
my father freshly dead this month.

I sit on the floor cutting out a pumpkin
for the children. I am trying to remember
how long it is before a cut pumpkin begins
to rot, to soften and grow green and black
mold around the eyes and mouth, how long
before it loses its body and begins to sink
into itself.

I have no feeling for this pumpkin
with its ridiculous round face, bloated and orange
as my father's. I cut into the firm flesh,
I make the face up as I go.

2

The thing is, I am my father.
I look at our face,
the smell of pumpkin in the air,
and I feel him in me like a great thirst.

I cut and scrape, cut and scrape, shape
the face of the pumpkin, place a candle
inside to light up its empty center,
fit the top on like the lid of a coffin.

Grief

The world is gray with grief:
one hand sobs into its twin its sorrow
at that very twinning; the coffee that wakes
us to the world pools its bitterness into us—
we will drink black lakes of it before we die.
The pen grasps for joy but never quite reaches it.

I try to remember the positions of desire,
the involuntary opening of the mouth, the wetting
of the outer lips, the quickening of the finger-pulse,
as if by remembering one could will the body well.

The table moans under the weight of its mortality;
cups cry, their mouths stretched open
in despair—they know they will be washed
regularly, only to be filled again,
emptied.

Cars parked on streets
everywhere wait for someone
to get in, drive them
somewhere.

One does not see that the sky opens,
that trees moan with pleasure,
that life goes on without one's own

razored voice, one's throat swollen thick
with remorse, one's gutter-dark griefs gasped out
into the pungent, luscious day.

Some Months After My Father's Death

I am watching the movie *Twelve Angry Men*
because there is a character in it
who reminds me of him.

He is the one who wants to go to the baseball game
instead of decide on a man's life,
he is the weak one, the one afraid to reveal
what he really feels, the one for whom everything
is a joke. He is not Henry Fonda,
the tight-lipped moral one.

The man is despicable, his weaknesses obvious
to all, as obvious as Henry Fonda's goodness.
I watch the movie again and again, loving
the black and white of it, soothed
by the sound of my father's voice,
the careless pronunciation, the easy
shrugging of the shoulders at every crucial question.

I sink lower into the dark arms of the sofa.
Strange how comfortable the familiar is,
how we can even prefer it,
however terrifying.

Cajun

I want to take the word back into my body, back
from the northern restaurants with their neon signs
announcing it like a whore. I want it to be private again,
I want to sink back into the swamps that are nothing
like these clean restaurants, the swamps
with their mud and jaws and eyes that float
below the surface, the mud and jaws and eyes
of food or death. I want to see my father's father's
hands again, scarred with a life of netting and trapping,
thick gunk of bayou under his fingernails,
staining his cuticles, I want to remember the pride he took
gutting and cleaning what he caught; his were nothing
like the soft hands and clipped fingernails that serve us
in these restaurants cemented in land, the restaurants nothing
like the houses we lived and died in, anchored in water,
trembling with every wind and flood.

And what my father's mother knew:
how to make alligator tail sweet, how to cut up
muscled squirrel or rabbit, or wild duck,
cook it till it was tender, spice it and mix it all up
with rice that soaked up the spice and the game so that
it all filled your mouth, thick and sticky, tasting
like blood and cayenne. And when I see the signs
on the restaurants, *Cajun food served here*,
it's like a fish knife ripping my belly, and when I see
them all eating the white meat of fat chickens
and market cuts of steak or fish someone else
has caught cooked *cajun* style, I feel it
again, the word's been stolen, like me,
gutted.

Cleaning a Fish for the First Time

It was hard to actually make
the first incision. I don't know why,
maybe I was afraid of what might bloom
out under the blade, some dark mess
of guts or fish stuff, dark and creamy
as menstrual blood, or fish dirt
or fish fat that would get under my nails
like a smell.

I almost became hysterical,
holding the knife over the freshly dead thing
and thinking about it, maybe my brother
was in there, or a swollen eyeball,
a swallowed fish hook, Jonah,
a mutant God turned black and purple,
a heart—

I had to remind myself I was only
cleaning the fish, not killing it—
I had already done *that* dastardly deed,
given instructions from my sister,
expert in these matters, to hit it on the head
with something. She neglected to say
it was necessary to hit it *hard*
on the head, for to my horror
I found that, even after much hitting,
the gills still moved.

So I whacked at it again, harder this time,
until the gills leaked blood, thinking all the while
what kind of person am I. After a few more
whacks with a heavy board, my son said
I think it's dead now, mom.

My sister tells me she has seen
a fish gutted and scaled alive,
nailed by its head to a cleaning board,
the gills still moving. I have a new respect
for anything that tries this hard
to survive. Would we do as well,
weighted down in a river,
skinned, ripped open from the inside?

I wish fish would die as soon as they take
the hook, just float to the surface
already dead, almost like you didn't do it,
the fish line the distance
between the bomber and the bombed,
it almost wouldn't seem like killing.

This is what I think as I hold my breath
and nose against the possibility of smell
and cut across the fish's belly. What slides out
first under the knife is a small, perfect fish,
encased in a pink sac stretched thin and tight

as an embryo casing. *Oh mom*, my son says,
it was pregnant, and for a moment I believe
too—not only am I a fish murderer,
I am the murderer of a pregnant fish.

Then I remember. *No*, I say with a calmness
I don't feel, *it's just a fish the fish we killed
ate.* Oh, you mean it's part of the *food chain*,
my son says, emphasizing *food chain*
in a way he has that means it is something
he learned in school. He wrinkles his nose,
scrambles off his chair, disinterested now,

the theme song for other mutant killer creatures
calling him to more important matters of the television,
leaving me alone with the split fish,
its guts spilling out like pearls
into swiney hands I do not recognize.

Too Late, for My Fingers

I understood it today, with that stupid kind
of understanding that floods over you like some
low-watt bulb, an arthritic hand slowly
turning the dimmer up, that the soreness
in my fingers would not go away,
it would stay like a new husband
and grow fat, spread to other fingers,
reproduce itself in my hand, the fingers
curl into tight claws, the hand itself
become the stiff shred of a flag.
I want to argue with someone about it,
file a complaint about distribution of genes.

But mostly I want to apologize to fingers,
too late I want to celebrate them,
pamper them, write odes to them, take back
every moment I took them for granted, tell them
how long and lovely they are, how I am filled
with the beauty of fingers, how the soul lives
in fingers, how the life-grip is in the fingertips.

I look at them, curl and uncurl them, stretch
and reach until I think the hand will split,
remembering the impossible stretches of youth,
the contortions of correct finger positions
for guitar and piano like those of early
love and sex, full with the belief
that your fingers can play any chord or arpeggio,
pluck any melody or bass line. Later,
the fingers typed me through graduate school,
and I worked hard to strengthen my grip,
and my marriage, to make firm my hold
on my husband, as if the strength of the grip
were everything.

The fingers themselves are wise,
they wear their knowledge like scars.
I have cut them, burned them, hammered them,
I have curled them gently around the penis,
taught them to love the curl,
I have stuck them down my throat to tickle
the gut up, they have gripped my son's hands
to pull him from death more than once,
they have spoken for me when mouth
could not, they have gripped pen
with strength when will could not,
and I will miss them, would rather my face
go ugly and peppery, let the cancerous moles
push their snouts up through the skin
than lose this, my grip, my scratch,
my intelligent clench.

Eating

I have eaten the blueberry pancakes with their rich wells
of butter and syrup, and I have not once thought
about the weight of syrup and butter on heart and hips
already heavy with living. And the crisp, hard bacon,
all four pieces have I eaten, and not once have I thought
about the pig's sufferings, but have enjoyed
the beautiful slabs of fried fat, have taken pleasure in the eating of it,
as someone may take pleasure in the plumpness of me.

How could I *not* eat the pancakes with their blueberries
like eyes that bleed blueness everywhere, the fork,
the plate, my lips and tongue stained
with the greedy juices of ripe blueberries.
I want to forget the sad tuna fish sandwiches
and cottage cheese lunches, to hell with the idea
that I could be slim, happy
without pancakes and syrup, butter and bacon.
I'll take hips full and wide as the earth, legs big enough
to swallow the night, a body that shouts the pure delight
of eating, the meat of the earth, the sweet and salty
fruit of the earth. Let me die with a syrupy grin
and bacon breath, blueberry juice
inked thick in my mouth.

On Taking a Child to Your Bed

Dr. Spock says don't do it, let the child cry
all the endless night, let him cry
into the mewling darkness where
all unanswered cries of children go,
but do not take him back into that
place of his making. My mother must have learned
from this man, or else she sensed more danger
from their bed than the predators of night,
for we were never taken there; though we called
their names, our cries flew over the house
on the wings of black angels. We punched
pillows, hugged our emptiness, slept in our separate dark.

And this is how I learned to sing, to place some song
against that motherless, fatherless black.

And now, when my son wakes from some dream
of loss or terror he cannot describe,
I take him to the bed my mother never let us lie in,
the bed with its daily sweat and sheets,
its smells of sweet sex and washed blood.

I wish my mother could know this joy:
how I hold this small child against my body
to warm him, how he spoons himself
back into me and out of nightmare,
how my lover holds us both and we fall
into sleep, back to the first deep cave,
the first fire, the first song.

Wanting to Be Mary Magdalene

It was because I believed everything
they said about her before
she met Him, she spent her nights
in dark tents opening
her legs, her body
washed and oiled and smelling
of musk, the hair
under her arms, on her legs
and between her legs thick
and fragrant, and her breasts
were large and full, and usually bare,
and she laughed and was pleased with herself,
and went through the world uncovered,

and when she met Jesus
she loved him the only way she knew.
She did only what he allowed
though fire rained in her like Sappho:
when she knelt before him
to wash his feet a pungent smell
rose from his groin, hot and untasted,
and the sweat and dust on his calves
was thick as honey, and his feet
were almost black with walking,
callused or red and raw
where the ill-fitting sandals
had rubbed, and she washed
and oiled his feet as she did
her own body, and wrapped
her long hair, thick as a towel
and more reliable than any god
around his feet to dry them

and that is why, when they confirmed me
into that pure Catholic world
and asked me my new name,
I gave them hers.

First Summer in Nice

Sometimes I see a woman who looks like her
with lips full and intelligent, and my own lips
begin to ache like they did that summer night in Nice
as I listened to her talk, watching her lips
as if they were filled with heating milk
I couldn't let boil over,
realizing slowly and almost without surprise
that I wanted her lips,
wanted to take her language into my mouth. Instead
we spoke a language neither of us knew as native,
a language as foreign to our mouths
as what we did with each other.

We lived as if drunk all summer;
we were young and heady with speaking and dreaming
that language neither had spoken before,
and the country was kind to us,
not caring that we held hands,
that we kissed not caring,
that we bared breasts in public sun not caring.
We swam unclothed in the ocean for the first time,
and the sun was generous and bright as our love,
as the discovery that breasts lose all heaviness
when loosed in water.

But I could never give myself up wholly to it;
some part of me was always watching us, observing
even as I loved that this was what it was like
to love a woman. And even as we giggled how well
we knew to please the other, gift of having the same body,
we talked about being mothers.

I finally pushed her away, the lips I loved
I made to quiver. I knew we couldn't stay
in Nice forever—we would have become crazed
with each other, not knowing how to proceed,
at each step sure the earth would swallow us up.

These days, safe and sane in my own language,
I sometimes hear women whispering in the halls:
I could never kiss another woman, could you?
their mouths screwed up as if they had eaten
some rotten fish, and I wonder do they think
you can do anything about it when lips of woman
or man ask to be kissed, when love
calls out in its strange and generous language.

Eating Raspberries

feels beautifully unholy,
the warm berries small
hearts or bits of tongue or lips or
the sweet balls of some man you love.

I roll one around in my mouth,
try to get the tip of my tongue
into its center of emptiness, the space
where a tooth was once rooted, the berry skin
around it like soft gums still in shock
that the tooth is gone.

I hold it in my mouth without biting,
like a Host: I believe in raspberries.
They are like us—coreless—it is what
surrounds that matters,
the infinite variety of berry skin
and berry hair—
blond stubble on a man's chin,
the tongue's cilia, frozen
sperm, hope.

I love the season that gives us raspberries
soft and brave in their boxes, *come*,
they whisper in their raspy voices,
bite, our seeds will crack bitter
as loss under your teeth, our juice
will coat your tongue, pulpy, sweet
as human blood from some mortal wound.

HOW
HEAVY THE
BREATH
OF GOD

1994

Looking for Grace in Ecuador

I am looking for the archangels
of my childhood, their pink
fleshy wings like candy,
the nimbuses of saints, gold as pollen,
the holy mothers of children,
the carpenter father,
I am looking into the soupy
eyes of dirty children,
god strapped to their backs,
I am looking for the grace
to wash sight away.

Street Market, Otavalo

The first thing you notice is
the air smells different
and you are afraid of the smell
of street and rain and exhaustion
and the large weeping of mountains
and the ancient sidewalks
with their ancient smells and ancient cracks
and pools of water that smell
like broken pieces of lives,

so you step over the pools
afraid to look in them
and still there is the smell
ever rich ever growing,
feather and chicken tied for selling
smell of blood and meat,
the stripped flesh hung from hooks
in the street like tapestries
and boiling chicken smells in the stalls
and roasting pig and guinea pig and lemons

and bananas and limes
and the smell of wood, fresh
and damp and older than you
will ever be, and there is breath
and skin and color everywhere.

And you stay outside of it for a while,
afraid of the colors and the faces
too pure, dark as those pools
of standing water in the broken
sidewalk you will not look at,
and then you see your own face
in a window, pale and washed out

as your life seems, less than a shadow,
but still you are afraid
to breathe too deeply for fear
of what might enter unseen
into your small completely insignificant

white nostrils, what sex, what
disease, what death, what
unwanted desire.

But for no reason at all, certainly
not out of bravery, you walk into it
anyway, and when you see the first brown breast,
the first woman and child,
the dark nipples like pieces of dark gold,

it takes your breath away, the pure brown
against the pure white blouses,
and when you see the next
and the next, the large bodies,
the large breasts,
it seems the milk is running
down the streets, rivers of milk
and suckling children,
and the backs bent and loaded
with children and wool
and on every street women
give themselves to children
like wild fruit. Some children lie spread

across the laps of their mothers
sleeping but holding
the nipple tight in their mouths
as if it were a dream,

or candy or God, and you forget
to think about not breathing
and it all enters you, the smell
of wet straw, exhaust
of cars and broken down buses,
the sweat and breath of foreign bodies
and even the smell of wool enters you,
and the smell of money
and hands old and cracked with barter
and the smell of beggars with faces

so mangled they no longer look like faces
but puzzles put together
the wrong way, so that
you cannot look or breathe again,

and you cannot believe there is a god
until you hear the words, *granadillas*,
semillas, *naranjas*. You are beginning
to notice how the clouds are sinking
into the Andes, the mountains
with their strong backs
and eyes like stones or stones
like eyes, you can no longer tell
which, and without warning
Christ is paraded through the streets
painted and bleeding
and pierced, the nails clear
as the smells now, it is

the Christ of your childhood
all lit up with flowers and lights
like a Christmas tree,

there are singing people
and dogs and a band,
sellers and buyers, backs and hands and breasts,
and long after it is all over
you are still standing there breathing
the thin night air,

and there is only one man left
with one flute, his black hair
pulled back and braided to the waist.

He is standing in a doorway to a place
you cannot enter,

and suddenly you notice how high
the clouds have taken you,
how the sky sings, how
heavy the breath of god.

Why I Went into the Jungle

Because I wanted to become blind again,
as at birth, because I wanted to feel
darkness heavy and wet around me
like sex or death, the molecules of night
dancing in my skin like jaguars.
I wanted to lose my way
to light because truth
loves darkness, I wanted to be
where I didn't know the names
of things to learn them
as blood learns the way of veins.
I wanted to fall into the malarial waters,
to be born again, a thing alive
and dark with knowing.

What the Sea Turtles Know

The mothers know to come out
of the sea under cover of dark,
they know to bury their eggs
under sand, and the turtle
embryos grow in that dark,
learn it as I have not yet learned mine,
suckle it in place of a mother.
Lain and warmed to being
there, they know to wait for night
to be born to the sea
where their kind await them.

I have seen frigate birds and hawks
circling for hours the great nests
of sea turtles on days
when clouds chum and joke
with the light, so that day
seems night come early
and hatchlings make
their fatal mistranslation
of light and rise from their nests
thinking to make it that short way
to sea, only to be plucked into light,
into clouds, accomplices
of that grinning murderer, day.

The ones who wait for the real dark,
the ones who make it to the sea,
know that darkness is all desire
and that desire, life—
and so they return

to the waters of the seas
where they were conceived,
to lagoons lipped with mangroves
their roots hard and straight as bars,
and there the turtles love
and mate in their own way.

Creatures of light,
we do not see much of them,
only now and again their huge
intelligent heads that lift
out of waters for the briefest
of breaths, only the trails
the new mothers leave
from sea to nest and back,
the way between their thousands of eggs,
their wondrous dark.

In the Garden of Eden

No one tells much about it,
but there were vultures in the Garden of Eden,
Turkey vultures, to be exact.
Dark eagles, they would soar like gods,
voiceless, their wings held out in blessing,
their unfeathered heads the red jewels
of the sky of the garden.

They were vegetarian then.
There were no roadside kills,
no bones to pick, no dead flesh to bloom, ripen.

And they were happy.
They could not imagine
what they would become.

Big Fish

The ones that grow large and thrive,
the ones that have once tasted the hook,
the mouth-scarred ones, do not linger
in unclouded waters. They have learned
to live in deeper pools,
water cold as knives, weedy
with dark food, murky
amniotic fluid—

Wise fish, with gills
that open like wounds,
passing the tragic waters
through their bodies,
turning grief to oxygen.

Fisherman

To listen with hands and eyes
for the deep, unseen, mouthing—
if I could have the faith of the fisherman
I would rip out my heart muscle,
sink a hook into its joyous pulsing,
sing it out on a long line,
and wait for the great dark.

The Headlights of God

The world is still dark
with night's wisdom
but for my headlights,
which light the dirt road ahead
like God's shining.

A rabbit trips
into the light, bounds ahead.
He bounds and bounds, faster and faster;
we follow in our car. Sometimes
he stops to look behind,
then bounds ever faster ahead.
My son doubles with laughter,
urges me to drive faster.

I think how heavy the rabbit must be
with terror—he has forgotten
or can no longer see
the dark brush on either side,

he has forgotten or has not yet learned
that the thing lighting the way
is almost always the thing
from which you must escape.

Losing Faith

Her robe was sky on a spring night,
edged in gold, it hung on her
in folds that sighed about her body.
Her face was all I knew of beauty
then, flawless, earthly,
with flushed cheeks and peach-dark lips
open and almost breathing,
giving and taking back at once
hope.

Her hair was the color of young oak
and fell in waves around her face
where it disappeared like God
into her mantle. The folds of it
and the robe met at the neck,
and I loved this small mystery about her.

She stood on a globe of the world
and was queened with a moon
the color of honey. Her eyes were blue,
cold and warm both, her feet were bare,
naked-pink, and crushed a colored snake
that muscled about the world.
There were always candles lit
at her altar that gave off
a burnt perfume I loved.
If I crossed my eyes
they looked like stars.

I will never forget that Sunday
we arrived for mid-morning Mass
to find that all the statues had been washed
of color and painted brown.
The priest explained it was to remind us

they were symbols really,
that we had been taking these statues
much too seriously, that we needed to remember
they stood for something beyond themselves.

It was never the same after that,
the poor washed brown of her statue
reminded me of roaches,
or when we had to eat beans and rice
for a whole week once, or the generic
cans of peanut butter daddy brought
home from the army. I couldn't look
at her anymore.

And now, when I reach for the precise moment
of the larger doubt, its furtive dawning
in my child heart, the first knot of a wound
that would sing darkness awake,
it is the death of that statue I think of,
first sign that maybe what they had taught me
was wrong, that there were choices,
mistakes could be made.

Building for War

Imagine the moment between blindness and first sight,
a kind of color-fire you cannot interpret.
Hands are blotches of color with holes of light.
There are horrifying realizations—
that you have a face, an appearance.

A book about the wonders of eye surgery
also tells of unexpected failures:
a newly sighted man begs to have vision
taken away again, threatens
to tear out his eyes.

A cow bellows in the distance.
We sit on calm sofas, watch boys
with faces fresh as eggs
talk of war.

A cricket has been singing day and night
behind the refrigerator.
Soon he will drop from exhaustion.
It is dark black there, and warm—
he can not tell that it is day, winter.

Flooded Crossing

That month the rain was strange,
coming when we hadn't expected it—
ten cold inches during one week
in January. I had almost forgotten
what fear was like until we faced
the wall of shouting water,
swelling, flooding over the low
water crossing, blocking
the way to the house.

Stupid, I tried to ford the creek
at the crossing, refusing
to admit there was something
I couldn't do. The sucking water
turned me back before disaster,
but I stared for a long time
at my failure.

How could I tell my son what I saw
when he asked what I was staring at?
How could I tell him I understood
again, my brother, that last time
he pumped too much stuff into
his arms: the rushing of the creek,
something worth one's respect,
something to be afraid of.

August Fire

All that morning I had wanted to write about breasts,
pouting breasts, heavy and sweet with age,
or small breasts that tip upwards like swollen wine skeins,
young breasts ignorant of mouths,
breasts of new mothers hard with milk,
I had wanted to write about the weeping of breasts,
the scarring of breasts, breasts that smell of onions,
breasts that sway to the waist in joy or aching,
breasts that disappear to stretched skin,

so when I looked out the window at first
I didn't see flames but breasts,
their milk like fire in the hot windy air.
The heat that moved like a wall
was only the warmth of breasts on a cold night,
a place to keep hands warm.
Fire dressed the cedar tree near the house
then, like a lover, stripped it.
Flames licked the tip like tongues
would a nipple.

I don't know how long I saw breasts instead of fire,
how long it took me to phone for help—
when I finally sat down to write
it was night, my hands were black.

They tell me grass comes up greener
after a fire. I am happy to hear this,
for the land lies soaking in a black milk.

I look out over the waste of oak, cedar
and high brush and grass, my eyes
full of grief. Only the prickly pear,
that stout cactus, was saved
by its inner moisture. It bears
its red fruit like nipples hard bitten
and swollen. Its bodies, thick and green,
breast the blackened land.

The Erotic

I scatter corn around the yard and wait
for them to come at dawn and dusk,
two or three does together with twin
fawns, gangly, falling down. Sometimes
bucks come—alone, suspicious, male.
They are young, mostly. I watch them
in the dark of my own house
with binoculars, like a lonely woman
might watch a man undress
from a far window.

Bob says that the erotic
is hardly ever sexual, only
when we're lucky.
Oh how I want that luck!
I wait for the moment I love best
when their white tails go up
in warning, erect and full
as a loved one you stroke
but don't let come.

Want

Two young bucks come daily to eat.
Their nubs of antlers are almost
pushing through skin, it must hurt,
like new teeth almost erupting through
gums, the gums sore and red and full
of tooth. This is what it is like
to want you. Long days while
the gleaming white thing grows
larger under skin that weeps daily,
wanting to be broken.

ct Sex

Drones die after mating. . . .
After mating, male ants die . . . .
After mating, the female spider often eats the male . . . .
 —Field Guide to North American Insects and Spiders

Fabre describes the mating [of mantises], which sometimes
lasts six hours, as follows: "The male . . . holds the female in a
tight embrace. But the wretch has no head; he has no neck; he has
hardly a body. The other . . . continues very placidly to gnaw what
remains of the gentle swain.
And, all the time, that masculine stump, holding on firmly, goes
on with the business. . . "
 —Pilgrim at Tinker Creek, *Annie Dillard*

If there is a god, he is the one
responsible for insect sex.
How his divine brain must have
rippled like a big fish
when he thought of their writhing
at that moment of sexual prayer,
the fatal joining, the great
thrusting that is loss and gift.

He must have known that creatures
would evolve, that they would addict themselves
in time, to his dark symbiosis.

And he must have known that men
would become jealous of insects,
especially the mantid's fermata,
that they would fall, some of them,
into darkness, that they would invent
silk ties and belts for women
to wrap around their throats,
that they would close their eyes

perhaps as the mantid closes his,
at the moment of strangulation.

I remember that sometimes
when we make love
I am a host of god-thoughts,
crueler than any insect.

Poor insects, they have
no morals with which to dress,
only a mattress of indifference
to lie upon. They are bloodless,
and wear skeletons like coats.

Ours are hidden
under flesh and moral blood
that doesn't understand
its own dark rushing,
doesn't know how to say
without judgment
that there are places horrific in light
to which we swarm at night.

Blindfolds, Ropes

In this place of utter light and vastness
I have lit my soul with searchlights,
and cannot tell the limits of my fear or joy.

The truth is I miss your blindfolds and ropes,
those gifts I left with you.

In light you are gangly and red-nosed,
in dark you become the Beloved—
all breath, skin and tongue—
a truth no light would reveal.

Tonight when I close my eyes
the sky will fill with lovers
binding the wrists of lovers,
the night will tie its blindfold
over the earth's eyes, and I will
dream of how to speak—oh

kiss me with lips I have to imagine;
hold me in a room I can't escape.

Angels

Sometimes I think all angels are dark,
fallen like faith from the porcelain hand
of some god, all angels are angels of november,
of coming winter, of mutilations, addictions,
dead children and boys killed at war,
angels of mourning, they come singing dirges,
they are the ones who take grief into them,
it is what gives them shape, it is what makes them
so dark—it fills them like sails of ships that
will never return home, or bellies of women
who are pregnant and starving. I love how their song
floats down on clouded nights, that dark grace
like rain pelting the parched souls,
the empty tongues.

THE
JOURNALS OF
SCHEHERAZADE

1996

My Body in Summer

Not yet calloused, but cut and scarred,
bruised and dirty because I don't
wear gloves, am ungraceful—

I smell like sun, wine,
unstable weather, heavy rains,
peppers from the garden,
grass, new paint, like labor,
sadness, like a mother
who has lost her child,
weeds, tomato vine
ready to break from
the weight of tomatoes,

like broken
fingernails, finger
crescents of dirt, sex
without sex, like when a woman
removes her diaphragm
and smells the mushroom
smell of the gone one,

coconut, ink, despair, fern,
skin-grit, bruises, black flies,
who love my skin, it is a banquet
with its small wounds,
its salt and wine and smoke
smell from the barbecue,
my pungent armpits, fertile

as any forest,
sphagnum moss,
soft rotting wood,
the way river birches bend
until I think I will die of their beauty,

smell of everything I have touched
intimately and everything I have wanted to,
red biting ants, blood mosquitoes,
insect bodies that go flat like love
when we smash them,
all the small terrors we smell of,

hand of beloved,
milk, music and sky,
hope and veins, I am a feast,
a garden, a corpse,
my skin suckled and flayed,

and the late sun's death,
thick and creamy and dark,
covers my skin like a sauce:

from this have you come,
to this shall you return,
take this and eat of it,
this odoriferous perfume,
this blessed sweating body.

Rent

For nothing can be sole or whole
That has not been rent.
  —W. B. Yeats

The hardball came hard and fast,
not unexpected, but surprisingly
cruel to the one who ran,
face uplifted and radiant with joy,
his first baseball game,
arms outstretched as if in love,
just to the place where
his nose would meet the ball
straight on—

I heard the scream, saw him turn
around, the blood spurting out
of both nostrils as if every vein
and capillary in the nose were cut,
the blood pouring down the nose
into his mouth, the mouth filling
with blood and overflowing
to the chin, running down
underneath the Cub Scout shirt,
the dark red splotches turning
the gold neckerchief red
with blood's beauty.

I saw him put his hands to his nose,
cup it, pull one hand away
full of blood, *father take this cup*
from me, and I couldn't move
for a moment, though knowledge
continued to pour and run down his face,

though he looked screaming
at his palm, as if it were
the palm's fault, the blood darker
there and drying a little, now
filling in the fingerprints and life line.

It is my own hand, after the car accident,
I am in the back seat,
I have put my hand on my father's head
to shake him awake, I have pulled
my hand away, he has not woken.
I am looking at my palm, sticky
with the blood and hair of my father,
all of his mortality foretold
for me there in the blooded palm.

When one breaks a nose,
for that is what my son has done,
the evidence is in the X-ray,
the crack like a lost hair
there in the bone, the invisible
made visible. If only we could
X-ray our souls that way, find
the cracks, the cancers,
the evidence of love—
there, in my father's head,
that crooked line, that's love,
here, this other one, that's regret.

After you know the thing
is broken, there is nothing
to be done, you can only watch
the nose swell and poke out

where it shouldn't,
open and blossom
like a flower that doesn't
want to die, its petals open beyond belief
for days after cutting, as if the very act
of cutting has brought on its most intense beauty.
My son looks at himself in the mirror,
fingers the bruised and broken
thing as if it were a hurt animal.
I think of my father's cracked head,
the palm of blood, the beginning
of knowledge.

Pain Killers

I love those drugs they give
to relax you, the kind gas
of the dentist, the mysterious
pills and shots before and after
surgery, you lie there
on the chair or the bed
like Christ, all your wounds
illuminated, vibrating
with existence:
        for this is what
those drugs do, they do not
kill pain, they illuminate it,
fertilize it, until you are
so aware that you are almost
numb, it is pain made so much
itself it doesn't seem like itself.

So there you are in the chair
thinking *I must cut the grass*
I must clean the house I
must read important books
and underline the important
parts, and then the drug
kicks in its sweetness

and your wrists that had been
tight with trouble, your wrists
that had shouted and shook
at your child, begin to warm and blush,

and your body relaxes.

You lie there
like nothing, the pathways
to memory opening, you can feel
the doors opening in all the veins
of your body, the first touch,
the first disappointment,
now you can stand to think
about it, now you can remember it,
despair, bitterness fully clothed,
sweet grace, you hold it in your body,
try to make it last,
close your eyes

and remember
how your brother would take
this sweetness, how he took it
and took it until his eyes closed.

Our eyes do not close like his. We
are lying down in an office, we
are waiting for a dentist, a surgeon
to cut us open, deliver us.

Hacking Away the Wisteria

The wisteria had become wanton, exuberant,
triumphant, almost hysterical, breathing its way across
my mother's lawn, working its way underneath the shed
through the floor, willing itself through the ceiling and out
the window to the holly tree on the other side of the yard,
wrapping itself around everything in its way, the azaleas,
hibiscus, camellias, all caught in its stranglehold,
insidious, another summer neglected and it would
enter the house, sneak its green fingers into my
mother's bedroom, surround her body while she
slept, enter her like some ancient god,

or my father—
We planted it together long ago, she says.
See how it poisons the ground, she says.

She had tried to kill it several times,
claiming it had responded too well
to the climate, that it frightened her—
it's like a thing
from outer space, she tells me,
and I see she is frightened,
she is thinking about her death;
every time I visit she gives me
some thing from my childhood,
tells me something I need
to know for when she dies.

So I become the kind of son
she never had, a noble prince, the hacksaw
my sword. I set to, hacking away at
the wisteria. I make a big deal of it, the way
we always make much of something
easy enough to do, so that

it counts in our favor when the harder thing,
which we cannot do, comes up.

How much, how much
do you have to cut off to begin again,
would we ever do it
if we knew what we nurtured
would become weed—

Afterwards, I place a piece of it
with root in a pot. When I leave,
the wisteria hacked down,
I take it home with me,
plant it in my yard.

I plant it
as if it were a piece of my mother,
as if it were a piece of my father,
as if it were my mother's slow death,
my father's gangrenous leg, his shriveled liver,
and I watch daily to see
if it's taken root,
I imagine it in my dreams,
the first push of new root into
soft fresh soil, moist with waiting, *wildness,*

wisdom, weeping, wickedness,
word, woman, wish, welt, wailing,
wanting, withdrawing, wet, within,
whip, willful, willing, wind there is

no wisteria in me, no wisteria,
there is nothing
my son will have to hack out.

Thinking About Being a Woman as I Drive from Louisiana to New Mexico

I am driving through the night,
dusk settling on the road ahead
like a tired woman,
I am driving,
a woman possessed,

and as I drive I think of how
when you have driven many hours
and are slightly deprived of sleep,
thoughts bloom
madly in you, uncontrollable,
like azaleas in spring—

I think of the bougainvillea
I left on a pot on my porch,
how the man at the nursery
had told me to keep it
rootbound, that it wouldn't bloom
unless it was stressed out, those
were his words, *stress it out,*

as if cruelty were a necessary
condition for beauty.

Blossoms
of lotus feet, hips hysteric
from cinched in waists,
plucked eyebrows, shaved legs,
curlers in the hair at night, headaches,
pin scabs from the plucking, rashes
from the shaving, the mothers
in China breaking the feet of their daughters,
wrapping the bones of the feet
in perfumed bloodied bandages
night after night, the men smelling the feet,

the blood in the East from the clitorectomies,
the women made more desirable,
the mothers do it, the blood
is on the mothers' hands, the cutting,
the girdles, the bras, the tight stockings,
the high heels, the corsets, the women
who starve themselves, the women
throwing up, the women being tucked
and stitched and sucked
and reshaped—

Rootbound. I say it
over and over again
to the darkening road,
as if some clue to my life
were there. What would it
be like, one's roots twirling
round and round in a clay
pot, dark and moist, nowhere
else to go but round, now
touching now winding
and twisting, but always
in the same direction,
around and in around
and in until the root
itself becomes soil.

You've got to suffer if you want to be beautiful,
my mother would say, though she hardly needed to tell me,
I could feel it everywhere around me as I was growing up
like the way you can sometimes feel the darkness
gets a texture, takes shape, touches you all
over your naked body at night.
The girdles and longline bras
she spooned herself into, the first bra

she strapped me into . . . that
was the first time she said it to me,
reminded me of the little mermaid
who had to attach clams
to her tail when she turned fifteen.
It was in all the stories though, the sisters
who cut off their toes and heels to make
them small enough to fit the glass
slipper, the blood
filling the shoe like gold,
mirror mirror on the wall
who is most beautiful of all—

The night lies on the road
ahead, a rich carpet
or a tablecloth, or a sheet
I have to change,
and sometimes I wish
I could shake off my mother's sex
like a bad dream. As the hours
stretch and the dark becomes
darker and the fellow travelers
become fewer and fewer
and almost hallucinating
with lack of sleep and
pumped to exhaustion with
caffeine and sugar, I think
of how, like this, one can sense
the desperateness of night,
how a certain kind of music
could drive one
to almost anything at night.
I understand how murders
could be committed at night
by those perfectly sane in the day.

The way night enters you like a god,
Zeus and Leda, Europa, Danae,
Yahweh and Mary, like that—

My sister's friend,
raped last week in her car
by a man posing as a policeman
who pulled her over for weaving on the road.
I try to drive straight, watch
where I'm going, not to break
any laws.

The time in Costa Rica
alone in the tent by the volcano,
the five men drunk
coming to swim at midnight,
stripping naked
in the moonlight,
the way I
clutched my knife
and didn't
sleep that night.

The time in New Orleans
the man who turned my
electricity off, waited behind the bush,
pulled the belt over my throat,
my voice, my scream all that saved me,
the gun I finally bought in Texas.

Maybe it is now that the animal,
armadillo, possum, something
large and slinky, appears
in my headlights like a messenger
from the night, already under

my tires, no time for swerving or stopping
or thinking. I hit it straight on,
sixty miles an hour,
feel the thud of tire against body,
feel the car lift a little like hope
then fall, then the back tire hit
and it's over. I'm gone.
Two cars behind me. Was it
hit again, and again? Was it
knocked over, back broken?
I don't stop, I don't go
back, what if I had a gun now,
would I be like a man,
would I go back
and see what I killed? Would
a man go back? I keep driving,
gripping the steering wheel, now ready
for any kind of light on
the horizon, almost not breathing,

I have killed something,
but I keep driving, that is all
I know to do, keep driving,
roots ripped out and flying
back like streamers or bloomers
or bras, I am driving
away from and into my sex,
my light.

Sestina for the Beloved

I would wake at night to their breath,
the sound of them together, their want,
the smell of their thighs and bones,
even thousands of miles away I could feel him undress
her, could hear his voice speaking
her name. It is not my name, which is difficult.

What he had with the two of us was not difficult,
it was as easy as night's breath,
as easy as me not speaking,
not saying what it was I wanted
most, not saying I wanted to undress
only for one man, only for one to know the bones

of me, the bones of my mouth, the bones
of my feet, of my heart, even the difficult
bones of my eyes and sex, only one to undress
my voice, only one to sing my breath,
only one to know the forest of my want,
to know there is only one who is speaking

my name in dreams, speaking
my body as if even voice had bones.
What I want is uncompromising, what I want
is difficult,
is like wanting water to offer breath,
is like wanting fire to undress

itself, is about possession undressing
itself, is about what it means to be speaking
at all, is about belonging like breath
to the beloved, the one whose bones
are inside you like so many difficult
hearts, the only one you want to want

so much that all there is of living is that want.
I cannot tell you it will be easy to undress
your heart only for me, that I will not be difficult,
that some days and nights you may feel as if you are speaking
to no one, that some nights your bones
won't ache for the touch of another, the sweet breath

of the unknown, the undressed breath
of one less difficult, a bone-
want that I will recognize, whose ache I will honor and sweeten
    with my love, my many, many breaths.

from Eight Nights of Fantasies

The First Night

The Invitation

It is August and even the moon
is hot, a white cake
baking in the night.

Two thousand miles gone,
how to bind him, how make
him taste this cake.

This is my canoe, we
are paddling into the moon
slipping over warm-worded
water like black glass, under
sentences of cypress trees hung
with gray moss lungs
of stories never told.

The night is sex, a woman
with full thighs, a woman
who smells of apples, a woman
lying on her back, carnal
mushroom, the air
is heavy, the hot weight of a man
you can taste,
his hands smell of garlic and wine,
his breath is food, I want
to devour him, I am paddling,
I am undressing into moon,
this is an office, this is a bedroom,
this is a boat, this is a baseball field,

this is a church, a card game,
I can take or be taken, I can
punish or be punished, I am she
who tells stories to stay alive,
come to me and I will let you wrap
a rope around my wrists and I will tell
what I dream, what I breathe,
what I think when I bleed, when I come
in the mouth of the moon.
Roped to night, I will make
this the rope that binds you to me.

Hot and glowing like trust
moon's blood-light will cover us.
We will paddle into it,
and we will breathe.

The Eighth Night

In The Galapagos Islands

I am brown wheat
the sun hot in my body,
I am lying on top
of a small fishing boat,
I am wanting to be fucked
by the sky, as if it could gather
itself into a shape,
I am thinking of the quickness
of the birds' mating on the islands
how I don't want that,
I am thinking of the long scar
on the leg of my guide from the macho
sea lion, sinking its mouth into
her flesh, to be bitten like that,
is that what I want, and the otherness
of these animals and plants—

and could sex evolve into something
wholly other here, could one come
to me as sky or ocean, as emptiness,
as thought, as animal, could I
embrace this sun that made me brown,
could our mating
become these islands,
volcanic isolate teeming
with beauty, strangeness.

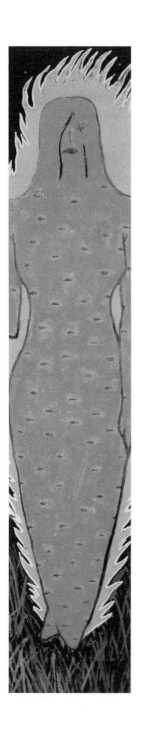

NEW
POEMS

Snow Storm

The snow falls, freckling the sky
with flakes as beautiful as any
in a child's storybook. It falls and falls,
and as you watch, housebound, day after day,
the layers of snow grow on the ground
as a life does, almost imperceptibly,
until you stick a shovel into it
to make a path somewhere and see
that it is two feet deep and hard
to move. And as you struggle
through the coming days to keep
the way clear, you begin to understand
how too much beauty can be deadly.

When you look out your window
everything that's not snow seems ugly—
gray and dark, slushy and messy,
not like the snow, glistening and sparkling,
pure and white, untouched by us—

but it's the ugly parts that are the paths,
the streets, the way the hell out of here.

Snow: Six Months Sober

Snow deepens the color of most things save me,
its brightness, like some fulsome sun or song, floods
whatever it touches. Because of snow, I see
the maple's bark is the color of old blood.
Snow hurts; its whiteness reveals too much,
makes too obvious the separateness
of things. There's nothing it doesn't hurt to touch;
a truth hands stronger than mine might miss.
It is unlike drink, which has its own duty:
to mash things together, a sweet paste; though
nothing is clear, all seems gorged with beauty.
But snow's all eyes, cousin of the sun's Apollo.
I was born dark and southern in snowless lands,
oh snow, daughter of a drunk. Please change my hands.

Midwestern

Rage, rage against the dying of the light.
—Dylan Thomas

Something about a landscape sober as this
brings out the Drunk in you, the one who drinks
to find fierceness, who drinks to feel,
who drinks because *this* is the path to ecstasy,
goddammit, that bright light of anger.
And as you drink and drink and continue to drink
you can feel its warmth tickling something in your gut,
something is unwinding there, where you were knotted
now you open, where you had no voice, or only a polite one,
now you are Godzilla, breathing a fire fueled
by rage. Now you can blame your lover, throw words
and fists at him, now you can hurl bottles of wine
at your books, which are stupid, watch the red stains
like omniscient ink blots mark their pages, now
you can blame your parents, too, worse than the books,
and your friends, anyone stupid enough to love you,
you can blame work, government, the gods, for this rage
you cannot own except when you are drunk.
In your blackest moments you even blame this land—
yellow-hearted and lily-livered—for not raging with you,
for not being as wild as you at the injustices it, too, has suffered
at the hands of these frugal, sober farmers.

Winter Solstice

Sometimes the dear ones disappear
despite it all, even though we can still
touch them, see them, they fall
into disaster, lost to mothers, fathers,
they are gone even to themselves,
though we speak to them as if they were still here,
the way you might speak to a comatose one
you hope will wake one day and say *I heard*
every word you said,
every one.

Other times they take even their bodies
away, they run, maybe out of fear
that the next arrest will land them
in prison, maybe they have argued
with too many, they have disappointed
even more, and so they vanish,
try to lose themselves to law
and the flawed ones who love them,
and who would also like
to disappear.

It's three days before Christmas, the sun
makes its briefest visit this day, it's minus
three degrees, and my son has disappeared
into the snow. Everything is fucked up,
he says, so he's taking flight, passing out
of sight, departing, withdrawing, quitting,
evaporating, deserting, and when I open
the door to let the dog out, the cold
slaps my face and the wind croaks out
the words I don't want to say out loud:
die out, dissolve, perish.

Promise of Snow

Thanksgiving break, and the city quiets,
seems half-full. Most have gone somewhere
else for the holidays. The cornfields
are empty, too, cleaned of corn,
and I've cleaned up too. The mirror
shattered when he threw my son
against it, and I've swept up the arrowheads
of glass, the ice picks, the tooth picks,
the thorns of glass, slivers so small
you don't notice them until they're inside you.
I've righted all the furniture too,
and scrubbed the dark, ruby-colored drops
along the stairs, the floor of kitchen and living room,
the smudges like blurred roses on the doorway
where he rested, like God before the seventh day,
and even the ragged pool of it on the bed.
I soaked and washed and bleached the sheets,
and all is white now, clean, like new snow,
what the weatherman promises for next week,
and sometimes I think that's why I live here:
because of snow, and the way it whitens and covers
everything: you don't even have to scrub. Slivers
and their sinister knowledge are buried under its crust.
You can believe, for a time, in emptiness, holiday.

A Few Days After the Attack

Because of yesterday's wind
all the leaves have blown
from all the trees in the yard,
for just this day the ground
is a mutiny of color.
Everywhere
I look I see my son's face,
the bruises blotting out his eyes,
his lips swollen black with blood,
his cheeks variegated: purples, reds
and yellows, the colors of a heart
torn from its chest. Here, in leaves
that blaze briefly then blur into land-
scape, the badges of the trespassed.

Wild Ones

Three times I have seen the one I love
cuffed and jailed. Arrested ones are always
loved by someone, the way soil
and weather love weeds, offer home
for roots, space and place to flower.

Coneflowers and milkweed, resplendent
and wild, thrive in my garden. Here
they are loved, though others poison them.
Farmers all around—everywhere I look—
lock the land up, box and fence it
to a form not natural. They want crops,
not weeds. Flowers of usefulness, not
flowers of evil.

The cop throws him against a wall
or door, jerks his arms back,
locks the cuffs in place in seconds.
They must train for this, like roping a calf
to see how fast they can do it.

And after they lock him up, your dreams
are full of cuffs—metal cuffs, leather cuffs,
invisible cuffs—cuffs upon cuffs that choke
and bruise and crush. There are heads and
hands and arms, but everything is necklaced
with cuffs. The cuffs are like gods:
you have no power over them. And him:
he is milkweed
and thistle, coneflower and violet, creeping
charlie, crabgrass, flowering dandelion. Neither
cop's cuffs nor your boundless love can save him.

Night

for my sister

1

Late summer ten years ago:
they are standing in shadows,
he reaches under her shirt
to stroke her breast.
It is the beginning:
his small hands feel cool
on her breasts, her nipples
ache like pennies
wanting to be spent.

2

Years later she will look at herself
in the mirror, hold her breasts
in her hands like gifts.
Now he says *they are too large,*
they do not fit my hands.
She lets them fall, and touches
her face, which he says he cannot
look at. She can't remember if
she is ugly or pretty.
There is a weight in her
like a stone moon. Mirrors
can no longer be trusted.
She cooks breakfast,
little sausages, fried in fat.

3

A closet is not such a bad place
to be. It is true there is nothing
to read, but since the light burned
out there has been nothing to read by.
There is a pile of clothes on the floor
that she sits on. The smell of it
is like a perfume of family:
greasy old slippers, the pepper
of vacuum cleaner dust,
wool and cedar, mildew.

She takes her ring off
and puts it in her mouth.
Metal and soap, it is something.
She can hear the children asking
their father again where she is.
Their voices seep like razors
Under the door.

4

She forgives him and sleeps with him
again. After all, there is the rent,
the groceries, the children,
her face—what kind of job
could she get with this face.
But most of all there is his
regular presence, like a light
bulb, there is his cologne,
which she loves, on his cotton
shirts.

She likes to sit up
at night after everyone is asleep
and breathe in his scent on the shirt
he has worn that day. First under the arms,
then the back. She buries her
face in it. A fist,
a kiss, one always follows
the other if she waits long
enough. They are the same.

5

Her friends don't understand
why she doesn't leave him.
She would point to his kindnesses,
which are many. She knows
the world is not black and white.
It is a bruise of splendid and various
blues, purples and blacks that stretches
as far as she can see.

The Night Before I Left for Seattle

I wore stockings because I know you love them
and you cooked mango shrimp. Knowing
I would love it. The dog was asleep on the rug,
Elvis Costello was singing something about
a house being empty, there was some recent
sadness between us lingering in the air
and after dinner we sat on the couch
and you opened my legs and looked
and looked and looked and we kissed
so long and so much and so deep
that the cold sore on my lip,
almost gone, broke open and still we
kissed with Elvis in the background
and Emeril muted on the TV and my black dress
hiked up and your eyes and lips on mine
and the knowledge of all that has passed
between us, and your hands on my thighs
and that red Cabernet in our mouths
and on our tongues and your sadness
at my leaving growing *please don't leave*,
you say, *I'll stop seeing her*,
and the knowledge that I have to leave
is like a virus spreading through me,
and if we must die let us die here, kissing,
your hands on my stockinged thighs,
the dog breathing steadily
on the floor beneath us.

Tinnitus

Don't listen, the doctor says
when I tell him about the sounds
I'm hearing in my newly deaf ear.
They aren't *real* sounds, because
I won't hear those again. The inner ear,
those thumbnail-sized canals
called cochlea and labyrinth, is destroyed,
and no sounds from the outside will ever
make their way as waves through
the sweet fluids of those bone-encased
sexy curves of tissue again.
No sounds from the outside will ever
wash like tides into my heart—no beloved
ever whisper or lie in that ear again.

Don't listen, don't think about it, the doctor says
when I tell him about the sounds the deaf ear appears
to be generating. Such intimate sounds,
I wonder that I never heard them before,
wonder if they were always there. Pulsing,
rushing sounds, organic sounds, someone breathing but not
me, not in tune with my breath, ocean sounds,
the sound a seashell makes when you put it
to your ear. I walk out into the strangely warm
November air, the sky as blue as an honest man's eyes,
into the small prairie back of my house,
and surrounded by waves of grasses all shades
of brown and blonde and red, it seems as if the sounds
in my ear might be coming from the land itself,
the language of these deep-rooted, dying grasses
the same as the language of my ear.

Don't listen, the doctor says. *People*
who have this can get lost in the world
of these sounds and disconnect from
the real world. Play a radio at night,
distract yourself.

But of course I don't listen
to him—I stay up nights taking notes
on what sounds I'm hearing. *Of course*
I listen to my newly wounded ear: I have
great respect for the wounded, they know
something about survival, and I want to hear
what my ear has to say, now that it's got my attention.

Sometimes the sounds are not organic
but mechanical—I hear microwave
ovens going off, that long beep
that announces your hot water or soup
or whatever you're heating is ready; or sometimes
it's that sound an elevator makes
when it arrives at a floor and the door opens;
sometimes it seems like the tones in an airport
announcing a forthcoming page: *poing* will
Mr. Howard Gold please pick up the white phone *poing*,
or the warning tone before a long moving sidewalk:
poing watch your step *poing* watch your step *poing*.
Sometimes it's like the bell on an old-time
child's telephone—*it's daddy calling!*—or
the bike bell going off, warning the lady
in front of you to get out of the way. Sometimes
it comes as a constant clicking pattern
that sounds like an SOS. Sometimes it's church bell
sounds; they are the most disturbing, because
I don't think I want to speak to God right now.

The sounds are constant, repetitive,
as if the ear, in its anguish at losing
its purpose in life, is repeating
all the sounds of a certain frequency
it ever heard, telling a story or narrative
of its life as an ear.
                    Don't listen, don't listen
the cold son-of-a-bitch specialist says,
but who could ignore such a wounded one
who comes with so many warnings and whistles,
bells and offerings? *I'm listening*, I say
to the swollen cochlea, the destroyed labyrinth,
I'm listening, even though I don't know
what ocean this is, what floor we're on,
what church or voice is calling.

A SUITE
FOR NEW
ORLEANS

Night Parade

These were the parades
where I sat on a boy's shoulders
for the first time, lifted
high and parentless above
the swaggering crowds,
where I gripped his head with
my thighs, listened for his voice
with my open legs,
waved for beads and coins
that were hurled at us like all
I knew of love then, the beads curling
over us like coupled snakes, coins
ringing escape on the streets,
the boy breathing hard underneath me,
and the slobbering grumbles
of motorcycles, like the first grunts of sex,
the first hardnesses felt in the first
groping darks, and the marching bands,
the mouths of their tubas and trumpets
shining and wet with our faces in the night,
and the floats, all lit up
and moving toward you,
your first and last chance
at something.

Jazz Sax

in memory, Lester Young

The way breath sings itself to controlled rapture
in the darkness of the bell, the way breath becomes shape

in the ear, sharp or slow, sly as syrup or sweat, something slurred
precisely.
The way the neck veins stand out blue and hard

when he blows, it's the sound of slow sex,
a tongue lush with love, eyes cool and shy with desire,

it's all the hundreds of muscles of the lips working together to
pronounce
some difficult word—it is wine and climax, heroin and thighs
open

for the first time, or again, and suddenly, after long closure,
it is vision, hunger, *yes* and *no* at once—

It is mouth as brain, its voice thick as god,
blowing fire and seas, secrets and seeds—

it is voice, metastatic ecstasy, the melodious
Snake of the garden.

Speaking About Loss

in memory of my brother,
André St. Germain 1964-2005

You have to say it: *Katrina,*
the water, unstoppable, the trees cut down
and speared into homes, the drowned homes,
the broken homes, the water lines, the mold,
the small dear things lost, the dead bodies,
the smell of decaying food and flesh. Dead,
neighborhoods you lived in, schools
and churches you attended, stores
you shopped in, homes you lived in,
people you loved.

And you want to remember the good, the happy times,
a gone brother laughing, a gone brother smiling,
a gone brother happy, playing with his kids,
boiling crawfish, grilling oysters for you.

And you have to write because poetry is best at howling,
it's the only way to say the unsayable:
that cities and brothers are not supposed to be lost,
that it feels wrong for them to be lost, that
you do not know what you are if family is gone,
that you do not know who you are
if home is gone.

And you keep writing even
though it doesn't seem to make things better,
even though it doesn't bring anyone or anything back,
even though the writing doesn't equal any of it:
the writing is like a drink you take
to be able to bear the remembering.

What We Found in Our Mother's Shed After the Hurricane

Broken tools, chairs from the sixties,
two broken bikes, a broken lawnmower,

eight moldy boxes of books, tax information
from the seventies. Lots of cat shit.

Piles of stockings, Maw Maw's walker,
Maw Maw's toilet, Mother's maternity clothes,

three letters to Santa Claus, lizards, roaches,
one dead squirrel, one unrecognizable skeleton.

Wisteria, mold, lots of sun.

Carnival: An Ode to New Orleans

So your house stinks, really bad, and the inside,
even the furniture, is covered with mold, it's like
everything has grown another skin, furry, yellow, black,
and you remember that sometimes when you walked
in the Quarter late at night you used to smell something like this—
a roux of rotting seafood, spoiled beer, and urine—
there's something almost familiar about the stink
of your ruined house, as if this is the base smell, somehow,
of the heart of your culture, the mold a mask
of something that was always already there.

Maybe your house has to be gutted, and you want
to hire someone to scrape the insides out because
you can't stand the smell or the pain of being bound
so intimately to this wounded thing,
but you can't afford to hire anyone, so you're doing it yourself.

Maybe the roof or walls of your house have fallen in.
Maybe your house looks as if it's had a heart attack.
Maybe a boat has knifed itself into the attic.
Maybe another house is on top of yours so that
it looks like the houses are fucking, and all of a sudden
you can't remember the last time you made love or were happy,
though you think of yourself as a happy person,
you are from New Orleans, born and bred,
how could you be otherwise,
                                  and you think you would like
to have some kind of hallucinatory, fierce sex with someone,
right this very minute, right on the moldy floor of your house,
you think you could loose your anger into it, empty
 your bruised heart into it.

Anger and sadness are boring, though,
and don't help with the gutting of your house,

and you think it might be better to make some gumbo
and light up the cave, like Ann Sexton says in that one poem,
instead of dreaming of having sex with someone,
and anyway there's no one around to have sex with.

And you're not so bad at the gutting,
it reminds you of eating crabs and crawfish;
you're good, because you're a southerner,
at cleaning crabs and crawfish, at dismantling them
and scraping out any piece of sweet meat that might be hiding
in any secret part, and that's how you have to hunt out
the mold now, it's how you have to scrape and pull
and be relentless. So you hold your breath and nose
and think about cleaning crabs as you work.

Maybe your house has drifted into the middle of the street
and has to be bulldozed because it's stopping the flow of traffic
of journalists who want to photograph your house. You think
about how hard the waters must have hit your house
for it to have been wrenched from its moorings like this,
and you remember how you felt after being punished a long time
when you were a kid and your mother finally said *okay now you can
go outside.* How you bolted, exploded out of the house.
You think the waters must have moved like that when the levees failed.

Maybe you've lost books or clothes or furniture or photo albums,
maybe you've lost a refrigerator, a stove, a computer,
your mother's wedding ring, your childhood piano.
Maybe someone you love has died.
Maybe you did not recognize the body when you saw it.

But it's spring, it's carnival, and you're sick of mourning
and sick of cleaning and gutting and sick of not having sex
so you wrap yourself in blue tarp and call it a costume,

and you walk around uptown with a sign that says
FEMA called, Beads will Arrive in April. Or maybe
you and your friends dress up like Dutch lesbians
and walk around with signs saying *New Orleans needs Strong Dikes.*

Maybe you put a toy helicopter on your head and disguise
yourself as a sand bag, or maybe you design a float
for your krewe called *The Corpse of Engineers*,
and you are almost happy.

Or maybe you just show up, as you always do,
dressed in jeans and a T-shirt, and stand around
on St. Charles, waiting for the parade.
Maybe you think it's important just to show up,
as if showing up proves you believe something
about this shattered city and your wounded house,
though you're not sure exactly what it is you believe,

and when the first float rounds the corner and you see the beads
whipping through the spring air, all that color and shininess
lighting up the sky, your heart almost stops,
it is like seeing someone you love again after a long, long time,
and you wiggle your way up close to the float, you put your hands up
and you yell as loud as you can, you scream, you shout,
you almost lose your voice, you are trying to get God's attention
or maybe just trying to get the attention of someone

who will make fierce love to you, *hit me, hit me
with some beads baby*, you're waving your hands
like you've been entered by a hoodoo spirit,
you got your mojo workin, you got your gris gris going,
hey hey hey, right here, me, me, you're reaching
for the roiling sky, for the beads that will change your life
if only you can catch them,

if only you can hear the sound of them
hitting your hand, hard,
the sound that means someone threw those
useless, shimmering, indispensable things
right to you, right into the palm of your hand,
and you are shouting for your house, for the heart of your city,
for the gone ones, *throw me, throw me something Mister.*

Bread Pudding with Whiskey Sauce

French bread goes stale quickly,
like all intensely pleasurable things:
brothers die young and beautiful,
a mother's smile disappears
to sorrow, passion dies to sex,

but sorrow can be transformed
into bread pudding. Break
the bread into small bits
as if you were a priest,
and this the bread for communion.
The prayer you will say
has to do with remembering
what it was like to eat it
on the street in Paris, a baguette fresh
from the boulangerie, a good
loaf, how it made all the day's pain
worth it, the crust brown and hard,
but not too hard, the inside soft
and white and cool, you could squeeze
it like a sponge, oh holy sponge
of God! it speaks, it sings
in your mouth, it fills you for
little money—

Scald milk until you can smell it, and the smell
enters your body the way it did
when you were a baby and your mother
put a finger between your lips
and her nipple to break the suction,
and in your sleep you could smell
the milk, still warm on her nipple.

The milk must smell like that
before it is ready.

The bread goes into the scalded milk
which will enter it like one who
cannot be denied, will transform
the dry hard pieces into soft moist bits.
Add raisins and peach halves.
Beat eggs with sugar and cinnamon,
freshly grind allspice and nutmeg.
It will smell like Christmas,
it will smell like your mother's
happiness. Mix it all together,
bake. The house will fill
with goodness, with the smell
of grace.

Make a whiskey sauce with brandy,
sugar, eggs and milk. Eat the pudding
warm with the sauce poured
over it. The raisins will be swollen
and full of the milky, bready juice:
they will burst open in your mouth
when you bite. The bread will be
warm and fruity, sweet
and spiced as you wish you could
make your life, the peaches will be
a surprise when you bite into them,
and the brandy cream will warm
you like sun, like sheets,
like your father's breath,
your mother's perfume.

If you close your eyes
you may almost be able to remember
summer, a pool of cool water,
the voice of your dead brother,
a smile on your mother's face.

Getting Rid of the Accent

I thought I had gotten rid of it
after I moved to Texas: speech classes
and twelve years in another state, but I'd
still fall back into it like into the gutter
whenever I visited, even on the phone,
whenever my mother called, forgetting
I was a college graduate, forgetting
I was an English major, saying things
like *wheah ya at sweethawt*, or
dat doan mean nuttn, ya awta seen
da way she pawks dat caw, the sounds
I was fed like milk as a child, the *aw*
sound predominating as if it was just
too much work to pronounce the *r*.

I tried hard to get rid of it,
to make my voice sound
as if I had nothing to do with
the black smell of the Lake,
nothing to do with my mother's
beans and rice,
nothing to do with my father's breath,
my brother's track marks.

Once, after listening to me speak,
a friend snickered, "I can tell
you're from New Orleans
by the way you say *room* and *leg*."
I couldn't hear it at first, couldn't hear
that I was saying *rum* for *room*, and *layg*
for *leg*. It was the hardest part
of getting rid of the accent,
rum still sounds more right than *room*,

gets the job done quicker,
with less effort. *Leg* was hard too
because *layg* was in me like blood.
It was a word my mother used a lot,
get your laygs off there, Sheryl,
close your laygs, Sheryl, wash
out the tub when you shave your
laygs, Sheryl,
                    but I practiced
and practiced it, the short *e*
of *leg* and the long *o* of *room*,
squinching my mouth
into the unnatural positions,
working my way from
the voice of my father,
the blood of my brother,

I was not going to sink
as my mother had, lower
and lower into this spongy
land, I would not have my words
sound like the drunken streets,
the ditch-water
that runs by our house still,
infectious, addictive,

when I sing of this place I love
unreasonably more than life
itself, I want the words to rise
strong and true, separate.

Joy

—for Teake

Some days we wake, filled with sudden song
at the body of the beloved
spooned next to us,
stunned at the way sun fills us
like butter, that there is wild mint
and thyme, sweet clover and honey
from creamy combs. There is desire,
there are the lips and hands
of the beloved, there is breath
and voice.

There are reasons for joy that birds
surely cannot know;
the moment before the pledge
that binds us to each other,
the moment our child
takes its first breath,
cries its first song of light,
and if we are lucky,
the moment even as one
slips to death.

Here we are so full with joy
that we cannot stop singing from tree
or fence post, here we are carried
by sheer happiness,
song thrusts us out to sky.

Design and Production

Cover and text design by Kathy Boykowycz
Cover painting, "Zydeco Diva," by Francis Pavy

Text set in Lucida Bright, designed in 1987 by Kris Holmes
Headlines set in Lithos, designed in 1990 by Carol Twombley,
    and Lucida Grande

Printed by Thomson-Shore of Dexter, Michigan
on Nature's Natural, a 50% recycled paper